MW01486942

Building Victory

Aircraft Manufacturing
in the Los Angeles Area
in World War II

This Douglas Aircraft Company machinist epitomizes the determination and "can do" spirit that has characterized Americans since the first settlers came here to build a home out of the wilderness. In this case, that strength of character helped win a war. (OWI)

Front cover: B-25 Mitchell bombers in final assembly on the North American Aviation assembly line at its Inglewood plant adjacent to Mines Field (present-day Los Angeles International Airport) in October 1942. Outer wings have yet to be added, and the planes are packed as close together as possible, resulting in the engine of one plane being directly adjacent to the next plane. (OWI)

Back cover: A Lockheed P-38 Lightning fighter is swung over a rolling cradle to begin its trip down the assembly line in Burbank. It will soon gain engines, wings and landing gear. Lockheed had never built a military plane before, but when it created the P-38, it produced one of the most revolutionary and successful fighters of the war. (OWI)

Building Victory

Aircraft Manufacturing in the Los Angeles Area in World War II

Dana T. Parker

Published by the author
Cypress, CA 90630
E-mail: jazzlover01@juno.com

Printed in the United States of America

ISBN: 978-0-9897906-0-4

Library of Congress Control Number: 2013910597

Notice: The information in this book is true and complete to the best of the author's knowledge. It is offered without guarantee.

As America's first giant of journalism, Ben Franklin, once said, our critics are our friends. The author welcomes comments and corrections regarding this book and may be contacted at the e-mail address above.

Dedication

To my children, who continually impress me. They have that same "can do" spirit that their ancestors had.

Contents

We won because we smothered the enemy in an avalanche of production, the like of which he had never seen, nor dreamed possible.

William S. "Big Bill" Knudsen
National Defense Advisory Commission

Acknowledgements

Composing this book has been a fun project, and a large part of what has made it such a pleasure has been getting to know the many estimable people who have been so helpful to me. Many of them work or volunteer in Los Angeles area air museums, and they exhibit the same pride in their craft that was evident in the people who designed and built these planes.

Of particular note are Ethel Pattison and Ed Crawford (whose encyclopedic aircraft knowledge both awes me and has been immensely valuable to me) of the Flight Path Learning Center & Museum at Los Angeles International Airport, Daniel Lewis, PhD of the Huntington Library in San Marino, Dan Ryan and Steve Benesch of the Museum of Flying in Santa Monica, Patrick Joyce of Northrop Grumman Corporation, Katrina Pescador, Alan Renga and Nelson Chase of the San Diego Air & Space Museum, and Cindy Macha, Barry "Herc" Smith and Ed Levy of the Western Museum of Flight in Torrance.

They have all been most generous in providing their collections, vast knowledge and their enthusiastic support. It is an honor to have worked with people of such caliber on this undertaking.

Dana T. Parker
Cypress, California

Photos as indicated below are courtesy of the following:

AAF	US Army Air Forces
FP	Flight Path Learning Center & Museum, Los Angeles, CA
HL	Huntington Library, San Marino, CA
LM	Lockheed Martin Corporation, Bethesda, MD
LBPL	Long Beach Public Library, Long Beach, CA
MOF	Museum of Flying, Santa Monica, CA
NG	Northrop Grumman, Falls Church, VA
OWI	Office of War Information (Library of Congress Collection)
PMC	Parker Manufacturing Company, Santa Monica, CA
SDASM	San Diego Air & Space Museum, San Diego, CA
SMPL	Santa Monica Public Library Image Archives, Santa Monica
UNLV	UNLV Libraries, Special Collections, Las Vegas, NV
USA	US Army
USN	US Navy
WMOF	Western Museum of Flight, Torrance, CA

Introduction

It was here – the Los Angeles area.

America's manufacturers in World War II were engaged in the greatest industrial effort in history. Aircraft companies went from building a handful of planes at a time to building them by the thousands on assembly lines. Aircraft manufacturing went from a sleepy 41st place among American industries to first place in less than five years.

The Los Angeles area was the center of this Herculean achievement. Douglas Aircraft Company was headquartered in Santa Monica, Hughes in Culver City, Lockheed in Burbank, North American Aviation near Inglewood, Northrop in Hawthorne and Vultee in Downey.

In 1939, total aircraft production for the Army Air Corps and Navy combined was only 2,141 planes. By the end of the war, America produced an astounding 300,000 planes.

In May 1940, Franklin Roosevelt stunned the nation by calling for 50,000 military aircraft. Hitler was reassured by his experts that this was just propaganda – there was no way America could produce that many planes.

Donald Douglas, president of Douglas Aircraft, heard the same speech, but he had a different reaction. His response was: We can do this.

And do it they did.

There has been no other six-year period in history when so many airplanes were manufactured. Production doubled, and then redoubled. The output of machine tools tripled. America produced more aircraft in one year than had been produced in all the years since the Wright brothers' first flight in 1903.

No war was more industrialized than World War II. This would be a war won as much by machine shops as by machine guns.

Manufacturer for manufacturer, factory for factory, worker for worker, the Allies out-produced their enemy.

Despite the massive buildup, an inexperienced workforce, and the inevitable inefficiencies created by the shift from civilian to military craft, productivity actually increased. Productivity in the aircraft industry doubled between 1941 and 1944. By 1944, each American aircraft worker produced more than twice his (or her!) German counterpart, and four times the output of a Japanese worker.

Who were these American workers? Largely women.

After losing thousands of workers to military service, American manufacturers hired women, to the point where a typical aircraft plant's workforce was 40% female.

In the First World War, the government had taken over the congested railroads. It didn't solve the congestion problem, and in some ways, made it even worse. In the Second World War, Roosevelt resisted the New Deal temptation for an industrial take-over. There was rationing of strategic materials, but, by and large, the government let business do what business does best: produce.

No company was told what to produce, or how it had to produce it. It worked. Production soared.

The profit motive proved to be a more effective incentive for production than government edicts would have been. In Germany, the Nazi generals directed manufacturing efforts (and changed their minds often). Germany's poor productivity was a reflection of this.

American manufacturers responded to the surging demand for military goods with unheard of alacrity. Even Joseph Stalin, the leader of world communism, praised American production, "without which this war would have been lost."

The US not only armed its own forces, but its allies as well. From a nearly standing start, the US produced over 300,000 planes. It averaged 170 planes a day since 1942, more than the Soviet Union and Great Britain combined. This industrial accomplishment ranks among America's most notable achievements.

In World War II, America produced an air armada that was the greatest striking force any nation had ever built. As Donald Douglas observed, "Here's proof that free men can out-produce slaves."

Where was the center of this remarkable achievement?

It was here – Southern California.

The Aircraft Plant

Shortly after the attack on Pearl Harbor, the phone of Phil Johnson, the president of Boeing, rang. It was Leonard "Jake" Harmon of the Army Air Corps. "Start building planes," Harmon said.

"How many?" asked Johnson.

"Just start building!" came the answer.

Naturally, a more formal ordering process quickly followed, but this urgent conversation illustrates the big picture. World War II transformed the aircraft industry from relatively small shops building small batches of planes to a truly mass-production operation. And, this metamorphosis was accomplished in a remarkably short period of time.

With small orders it makes no financial sense to invest heavily in the jigs and fixtures required for a production line. This level of tooling would reduce the labor required per plane, but with a small order, that labor saving is outweighed by the start-up cost.

So, from the early days of the Wright brothers all the way up to the eve of World War II, it made sense to make aircraft in a batch process (e.g., Perform one operation on all the planes, then the next operation on all the planes, then the next, and so on.).

Each plant was different, but as the war progressed, they moved more toward an automobile-like assembly line. Many new plants were built from scratch, and these, of course, took full advantage of the opportunity to set up an assembly-line process, some even with automated, continuously moving lines.

Naturally, this was not always feasible in pre-existing plants. And, for some functions, such as stamping out parts on drop hammers and subassembly operations, it made sense to continue with a batch process.

To the industrial engineer, three things were critical in designing an efficient aircraft plant: (1) Interchangeable parts (which meant they had to be made with great precision), (2) A smooth flow of materials (e.g., no backtracking), and (3) Balancing the line.

Precision and interchangeable parts are two key ingredients to the Industrial Revolution (which has produced the longest period of sustained economic growth in world history). A high degree of precision was needed, not just in engines, but in the rest of the aircraft as well, so that subassemblies would mate up properly when joined in final assembly. This meant that the jigs on which these assemblies were built had to be made to very close tolerances.

Ideally, a plant would receive boxcars/trucks of aluminum and other raw materials and parts on one side of the building, and the materials would flow through the fabrication process in a unidirectional flow until emerging at the other end of the assembly line as a completed aircraft.

However, different assembly processes take different amounts of time. What is referred to as "balancing the line" is the vexing engineering challenge to resolve this, so that the functions performed at the various stations on the line take the same amount of time. Adding more labor does not always resolve this problem, since only a limited number of workers can work in a given space.

Creative engineers came up with various solutions, such as setting up parallel lines for time-consuming functions, or otherwise changing the assembly process. For example, the Douglas plant in Santa Monica did both of these. It set up parallel fuselage assembly lines, and also built the fuselages in two longitudinal halves, like the halves of a hot dog bun. As much wiring, control cables, and other items as possible were installed on the two halves while they were still separate. This greatly increased the available work area and productivity, and helped balance the line.

Reconfiguring plants to achieve these objectives is easier said than done, and doing it without interruption to extremely ambitious production schedules makes it all the more difficult, but that was the challenge put to the aircraft industry's engineers. They met the challenge.

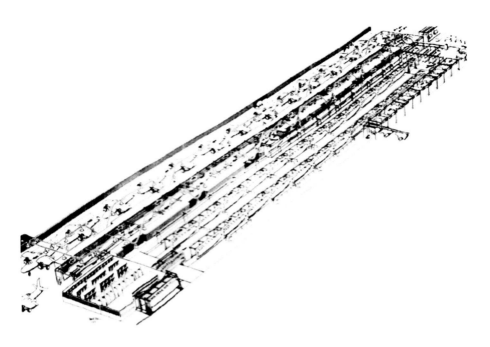

This diagram shows the layout of the Douglas Santa Monica plant's mechanized assembly line that produced the A-20 Havoc bomber. Fuselage assembly began on the bottom of the diagram on the right side of the building. Fuselages were built "on the half shell," which facilitated the installation of wiring, plumbing, etc. before the halves were put together. To balance the work time with other line sections, two pairs of fuselage halves were built simultaneously on parallel tracks. When they reached the other end of the building, they moved sideways to the left, then proceeded down the center aisle back to the bottom of the diagram, gaining parts as they went, and the two halves being joined together. They then proceeded back to the other end of the building, where they were mated up with left and right inner wing sections (which can be seen entering the diagram on the right side). Outer wings were added after the ships left the building on the lower left. Wing lines and fuselage lines moved intermittently. The main and assembly sections of the lines moved in a continuous flow. Stockrooms were adjacent to the work areas they fed, and parts were supplied to the stockrooms by a continuously moving overhead conveyor which would dip down periodically at points where its cargo would be unloaded. This aircraft assembly line, including its various feeder lines, was 6,100 feet long, yet fit into a portion of the building that was only 700 feet long. (FP)

This is the end of one of the fuselage lines at the Douglas Santa Monica plant. The two halves of the fuselage can be seen on the extreme left and right sides of the photo. Holding them are the large tubular steel jigs. Assemblers worked on the raised platform in between the two halves, as well as on platforms on the outside of the fuselages. (FP)

This view shows the end of the two parallel fuselage assembly lines. Reconfiguring the plant with this system brought the work to the worker, rather than the other way around. This eliminated the approximately 25% of the worker's time which had been previously spent moving tools, lights and platforms. With no increase in floor area, it enabled a production schedule which was 250% greater than the scheduled capacity of the building previously. (FP)

Douglas – Santa Monica

In 1908, with Orville Wright at the controls, the first US military airplane was tested at Ft. Myer, Virginia. Among the spectators was an enthusiastic 16-year-old who had convinced his mother that he *had* to witness this. His name was Donald Wills Douglas.

Donald Douglas had the drive and intelligence to match his fascination with flight. The second son of an assistant cashier at a bank, he won an appointment to the US Naval Academy. Douglas resigned though, and enrolled at MIT to become an aeronautical engineer. After being told that earning a bachelor of science degree would take four years, the Douglas drive was challenged: "I can do it in two years."

He did.

In 1914, he received his degree in aeronautical engineering, the first awarded by MIT. He then became the first aeronautical post-graduate student when he was invited to stay at MIT to develop coursework and build its first wind tunnel.

With his professor's recommendation, he was hired to be chief engineer for Glenn Martin Co., at the age of 23. The next year, he became chief civilian aeronautical engineer for the US Army. They waived the test for the position because there was no one in the country who knew more about aeronautical engineering than Donald Douglas.

In 1920, he came to California and established his first aircraft company office in the back room of a barber shop. The first plane was built in the rented loft of a planing mill (and brought out in pieces). The growing company soon had its own plant in Santa Monica.

In 1941, *Fortune* magazine wrote that "The development of the airplane in the days between the wars is the greatest engineering story there ever was, and in the heart of it is Donald Douglas."

By the end of World War II, in addition to its Santa Monica headquarters, Douglas would be operating plants in El Segundo, Long Beach, Tulsa, Chicago and Oklahoma City, with 160,000 employees. From a small company with only 68 employees in 1922, Douglas Aircraft had grown to be the fourth largest business in the United States.

Young Donald Douglas persuaded wealthy aviation enthusiast David Davis that Douglas could build a plane that could fly across the country non-stop. Davis invested $40,000, and they began in 1920 in the back room of this barber shop at 8817 Pico Blvd., Los Angeles. The plane was constructed on the second floor of the A. J. Koll Planing Mill building at 421 Colyton St. (below), and assembled at Goodyear Field. (SDASM)

The flight of Douglas' first plane ended in Texas due to engine problems, although it was the first plane to lift a load exceeding its own weight. Davis sold out to Douglas, who, in 1922, moved the firm to this building (an abandoned movie studio) at 2435 Wilshire Blvd., Santa Monica. The adjoining field proved inadequate as an airfield, so planes were towed down city streets to Clover Field (present-day Santa Monica Airport). (above WMOF, below SMPL)

Donald Douglas was a superb engineer and a bold entrepreneur. As the war approached he was also remarkably prescient. A year and a half before Pearl Harbor, he was already writing that this was the "hour of destiny for American aviation." He expressed confidence that the industry could meet the need, and he could see clearly how that could be accomplished. He provided details on each of the steps required: determining the types and quantities of planes needed, training personnel, establishing priorities in parts and materials, expediting machinery and equipment orders, overcoming bottlenecks, obtaining large orders of single types of aircraft to enable mass production, straight-line-flow assembly lines, subcontracting, and so on. It all came about. (SDASM)

Douglas succeeded in obtaining military contracts, and by the mid-1920s was a major aircraft manufacturer. Production went from six planes in 1922 to 120 planes in 1926. The company built a new building at Clover Field in 1929. Shown here is the firm's large hangar in 1938, with the center wing of an experimental plane, the DC-4E, being removed from its jig preparatory to being mated with the fuselage. (SMPL)

Riveters worked in pairs, one operating the rivet gun and one holding the bucking bar. The riveter pounded against the rivet's preformed head, and the bucking bar then formed the second head on the rivet's opposite end. Bucking bars came in a wide variety of shapes to fit in the many confined spaces on aircraft. The riveter and bucker traded positions from time to time during the shift. (OWI)

Unlike most aircraft plants, the Douglas Santa Monica plant did not have its own railroad spur. So, they used the Sunset siding, which was near the corner of Olympic Blvd. and Cloverfield St. Here they are unloading boxed aircraft engines onto a trailer to be shuttled to the plant. (FP)

This wartime view of the A-20 Havoc assembly line shows a small army of workers on a raised platform building fuselages. Just outside of the photo, on each side, are the other halves of the fuselages shown. The jigs holding the fuselages are made of welded tubular steel constructed to very close tolerances to ensure that the parts made thereon fit together when they are mated with other subassemblies later. (SDASM)

Life before the computer...

With pen and paper in hand, Douglas plant production planner Dick Besley looks up from his pile of work outlining production operations for the outer wing of a Douglas C-47 transport plane. (SMPL)

This is the inner-wing portion of the assembly line. With the sound of a whistle, a power winch would periodically move the line. From mid-1940 to mid-1941, the Santa Monica plant was expanded 30%, and employment increased by 70%. Mechanized track-assembly lines reduced man-hours required by 50% for some operations. Production tripled. (FP)

This is the end of the A-20 Havoc assembly line. Douglas' industrial engineers took advantage of gravity in this final section of the line. The floor sloped to the south, and here the ship rolls on its own gear as it leaves the plant. (FP)

The drop hammer was the most widely used tool for producing formed parts. A piece of sheet metal was placed on the female die in front of the operator's waist. The hammer (with the male die attached to it) would fall onto it, drawing the sheet metal into the desired shape. The hammer was lifted by ropes with several turns around a continuously revolving drum. The rope was wetted with water to reduce wear. A relatively light pull from the operator would be enough to lift the hammer, which weighed from one to five tons. A foot-controlled safety catch held it aloft, enabling him to change out the work. Often the two ropes were connected with a handle or lanyard, simplifying matters for the operator. He could snub the ropes to control the hammer's fall. Spare rope was held in spools on each side. (WMOF)

Prior to the war buildup, the Douglas Santa Monica plant was the largest aircraft plant in the country. It would be surpassed by others though, including by Douglas itself, when it built the Long Beach plant. These messengers in the Santa Monica facility photographed on May 12, 1943 used roller skates to deliver (at high speeds!) blueprints and other information through the plant, which was four city blocks long. (SMPL)

An organization the size of Douglas required a lot of printing. Shown here is the latest edition of the company newspaper, the *Douglas Airview News,* rolling hot off the press. (SMPL)

"Opportunity Day" was a way of showing prospective employees, particularly females, what aircraft work was like. "You can do this!" was the message. The riveter and her bucker have a large, interested audience for their demonstration. (SMPL)

The Douglas plant in Santa Monica was between Ocean Park Blvd. and Clover Field. After Pearl Harbor, the threat of an air raid on the West Coast was considered quite real. A Japanese submarine shelled an oil refinery at Santa Barbara two months later, making Californians even more unsettled. This entire plant, as well as others, would soon be camouflaged. (SMPL)

This is a view looking north at the Douglas Santa Monica plant after camouflage. Not only were the plant and adjacent runway camouflaged, but they even built a fake plant and runway slightly south of the real plant. The real plant is under what appears to be a residential neighborhood at the top center of the photograph. (SMPL)

This is a close-up of the residential neighborhood, complete with fake streets, trees and houses, made of burlap, chicken feathers and plywood. All of it is above the roof of the Douglas plant. Under what appears to be a gently rolling hill in the background is the company's large hangar. (SMPL)

Donald Douglas appreciated well before Pearl Harbor the likelihood of America being attacked, and that his plants were vulnerable to an air raid. Without waiting for protection from government, he took action. He put his chief engineer, a highly regarded architect and Warner Brothers Studios to the camouflage task. Realizing afterward that its studios looked a lot like an aircraft factory, Warner Brothers decided to camouflage its own buildings. (SMPL)

The workers in this photo and the barrage balloon in the background provide perspective for the magnitude of the camouflage task. The fake streets lined up with existing streets, and the Clover Field runway was painted green to look like grass. Even American pilots were confused and couldn't find it. They would then land at other airports and complain that someone had moved the field... (SMPL)

Douglas - El Segundo

Douglas Aircraft Company was the incubator for many great names in aeronautics. Jack Northrop is one of them. After working as a draftsman for Allan and Malcolm Loughead (pronounced "Lockheed" – they spelled their company name to reflect the proper pronunciation of their Scottish name), Jack Northrop went to work for Donald Douglas in 1923.

He was with Douglas until 1927, working his way up to project engineer. Northrop then left to join Ryan Aircraft, where he worked on the wing design used on the "Spirit of St. Louis," which Charles Lindberg would make famous by flying across the Atlantic. In 1932, Northrop and Douglas reunited to form Northrop Corporation, with Douglas owning 51% of the stock, and Jack Northrop 49%.

Northrop Corporation purchased a plant in El Segundo, where it developed planes such as the Northrop Gamma and Delta. The plant was just south of Mines Field (later known as Los Angeles Municipal Airport, and today as Los Angeles International Airport). Completed aircraft were towed down Douglas Street to the airport. It is said that the reason this short street was built so wide was to accommodate aircraft, not automobiles.

On-going union problems led Douglas to dissolve Northrop Corporation in 1937. The facility became the El Segundo Division of Douglas Aircraft Co. The entrepreneurial Jack Northrop went on to found his own company (the second Northrop Corporation) in Hawthorne in 1939.

During WWII, the El Segundo plant specialized in building Navy planes, particularly its leading dive bomber, the SBD Dauntless. The SBD (Navy designation meaning "Scout Bomber Douglas") is famous as the plane that won the Battle of Midway. The Dauntless was also instrumental in the victory at the Battle of the Coral Sea, and fought in every battle involving carrier aircraft. This ubiquitous bomber sank more Japanese shipping than any other aircraft in the war.

The El Segundo plant is still there today, and is still in use as an aircraft plant. It is now a Northrop Grumman facility, manufacturing center fuselage sections for the F/A-18 fighter.

This view is looking west along Imperial Highway, with Aviation Blvd. crossing it in the foreground. Los Angeles Municipal Airport (present-day LAX) is on the right. Along Aviation Blvd. on the left is the Douglas El Segundo plant, next is the Interstate Aviation & Engineering Corp. plant, then last is the North American Aviation plant adjacent to the airport. Douglas Street is just to the west of the Douglas plant. (MOF)

This hangar was just south of Imperial Hwy. and just west of Douglas Street. It was the first home of the Douglas El Segundo Division before moving to the larger facility half a mile east on Aviation Blvd. seen in the photo at the top of the page. After Douglas moved, this building became the home of Interstate Aviation & Engineering Corp. before it occupied its larger building on Aviation Blvd. (FP)

This 1936 view of the Douglas El Segundo plant shows how the small orders of the time were produced without assembly-line tooling, and the heavy investment it would have required. The relatively haphazard placement of these A-17 attack bombers is attendant to their being built on a batch basis, rather than an assembly-line process. The workers and their tools come to the planes, rather than the other way around. (WMOF)

With a yard full of SBD dive bombers looking on, Douglas adds a new building to its El Segundo plant in 1942. Barrage balloons can be seen in the background. (WMOF)

This final assembly view of SBD Dauntless dive bombers in 1943 shows how order size had dramatically increased. The perforated flaps were designed as brakes that allowed pilots to control their speed in a vertical dive. At Midway, Dauntless dive bombers left three Japanese carriers ablaze within a matter of minutes, and then sank a fourth one later in the day, changing the tide of the Pacific war. The hundreds of towering white posts supporting the roof of the plant were made of California redwood. (USN)

The engine line held dozens of Wright radial engines, which will soon be hung on the firewalls of SBD bombers being built behind the engines on the right. Wright engines were built by Curtiss-Wright Corporation, which was the corporate descendant of the Wright brothers' company. (OWI)

This is the interior of the El Segundo plant's main building, looking south in December 1944. A large press brake is in the foreground with racks of material on either side. A press brake bends sheet metal by use of a vertically moving beam whose stroke forces a matching punch and die together with the work in between. It is typically used to produce flanges, channel or corrugated shapes. (WMOF)

Often a riveter could neither see, nor hear, her bucker, so they worked out tapping signals. After feeling the bucker put her bucking bar against the rivet, the riveter would pound a bit, then stop. The bucker would signal, with typically one tap if the rivet  was good, twice if it needed more pounding, or three times if it was deformed and needed to be drilled out and replaced. (USN)

29

A new riveter is learning her craft on the wing of an SBD Dauntless. The jig not only holds the parts in the precise positions needed for fabrication, but also supports the wing in a vertical attitude which saves work space and allows the riveting to be done in a considerably more comfortable working position. (USN)

For small assemblies, a riveting machine could be utilized as is being done by Carol Angel in this photo. Small assemblies were made in batches, and were then brought to the assembly line as needed or were combined with other small assemblies to become larger subassemblies, such as a fuselage or wing section. (OWI)

The army of engineers in this photo of the Douglas Engineering Department in El Segundo gives a feel for the tremendous engineering effort involved in designing and building aircraft. Every part, every jig, and every fixture began as a mark from a 2H pencil on a piece of paper. (SDASM)

An invaluable tool in any machine shop, the drill press quickly produces accurate holes. Shown here set at 90 degrees to the spindle (and thus the drill), the table can also be tilted to produce holes at other angles. The machinist is holding the work here by hand, but it can also be clamped securely to the table or held in a drill-press vise, which rests on the table. (OWI)

Model maker A. P. Baldecchi was an international sculptor before the war. Here he is making accurate scale models to test engineers' ideas in wind tunnels. When Donald Douglas first came to California he brought with him two cardboard boxes containing the sum total of all of the world's aeronautical engineering knowledge. Thanks in part to wind tunnel research, by World War II, that knowledge had increased a thousand fold. (OWI)

Holes requiring high precision were first drilled. Then, the last few thousandths of an inch of material were removed with a reamer as seen here. The part here is being held in a three-jaw chuck, secured with T-headed bolts which fit into the T slots in the table. The flexible steel conduit at left feeds cutting oil onto the work, cooling the reamer and customizing the machinist's apron. (OWI)

The BTD-1 Destroyer torpedo bomber was built in El Segundo late in the war as a replacement for the SBD Dauntless and the Curtiss SB2C Helldiver. The plane proved to be much faster and could carry nearly double the bomb load of the Helldiver. It had tricycle landing gear, which was unusual for carrier-based aircraft. The plant's camouflage netting can be seen in the background. (WMOF)

These AD Skyraiders were designed late in the war as an all-purpose Navy attack airplane, capable of operating from all carriers, even the small "Jeep" carriers. The plane was designed to carry normal bomb loads of 2,000 lbs., but could also carry as much as 10,000 lbs. on short hops. The plane had dive brakes on the fuselage rather than the wings, and could be slowed down to less than 300 miles per hour in a dive for pin-point accuracy. (SDASM)

This SBD Dauntless dive bomber, freshly manufactured at El Segundo, is shown at Los Angeles Municipal Airport ready for delivery to the Navy. Visible beneath the fuselage is the bomb cradle (sans bomb), which allowed the bomb to pivot away from the plane, so that it would not hit the propeller when released. (MOF)

This dramatic shot shows an SBD dive bomber coming off the end of the assembly line onto wet pavement on a rainy night, ready to go win a war... (FP)

Douglas - Long Beach

Douglas Aircraft's largest facility was the Long Beach plant. Buildings here totaled 1,422,350 sq. ft., which was nearly as much as the Santa Monica and El Segundo plants combined. Advantages of the Long Beach site were its access to rail transportation and the port. Production efforts in the plant began even before construction was competed, and the first plane rolled out the door on Dec. 23, 1941.

It was the nation's first fully air-conditioned factory. Factories of the era had large banks of windows to bring light to the work floor. Not the Long Beach plant. Even though America was not at war (Pearl Harbor was still in the future), this was designed as a "blackout" facility, with limited, light-proof access, as a defense against the threat of air raids.

The Long Beach plant is a good example of the remarkable cooperation between the aircraft manufacturers during the war. They were fierce competitors before the war, and when the war was over, they knew they would resume the business competition that makes the free enterprise system work. For the duration though, they acted as brothers in a common cause: to defeat the Axis.

Aircraft manufacturers allowed their planes to be built by their competitors, even providing the licenses to do so at no cost. For example, Boeing's B-17 bombers were built at the Douglas Long Beach plant, and Douglas DB-7 Havoc bombers were built by Boeing in Seattle.

In addition, Donald Douglas arranged a meeting with the heads of the other Southern California aircraft manufacturers which resulted in extraordinary examples of mutual assistance in production. Managers of competing plants, who, prior to the war, had never spoken to one another, now would call their opposite number to swap or borrow parts, or even borrow machine time or exchange engineering knowledge in this unparalleled effort to get as many planes in the air as possible, as quickly as possible.

In one of the thousands of examples of this, Vultee Aircraft provided invaluable data that saved North American Aviation six months of engineering research on dive brakes. As Douglas observed, "that was six months gained on Hitler."

This view of the Long Beach plant is looking southwest with Lakewood Blvd. and Carson Street in the foreground. Behind the plant is Long Beach Airport, and Signal Hill dotted with oil rigs in the background. This plant has since been razed with the exception of the large hangar closest to the tarmac. Boeing (Douglas' successor company) produces C-17 Globemaster transport planes in a building west of the airport. (WMOF)

Step One in building the plant was building its rail spur. This allowed structural steel and other construction materials, as well as the facility's machine tools, to be shipped in by rail. Rail transportation is cheaper than truck, and more easily handles large items such as those seen in this gondola. (LBPL)

Douglas modified its remarkably successful DC-3 for military use with wider doors (capable of accepting a Jeep) and a reinforced floor, producing the versatile C-47 Skytrain transport. Eisenhower referred to this plane as one of the five most important pieces of military hardware of the war. The Jeep also made the list... (OWI)

The C-47 outer wing is not attached to the center wing with any kind of structural beam extending through the connection. Instead, a small flange is formed on the aluminum skin on each of the sections where they are butted together. A row of closely spaced bolts through the two flanges is all that is necessary to attach the wing. A fairing strip covers the flange, improving airflow. (OWI)

The skilled senior employees of the aircraft manufacturers were invaluable not only for their ability to produce quality work, but also to train the thousands of new employees, many of whom had never done mechanical work before. Many of these seasoned craftsmen kept working during the war, long after they would have otherwise retired. (OWI)

The stockrooms were just as capacious and just as busy as the assembly areas. One of the planes produced at the Long Beach plant was the B-17 Flying Fortress bomber. A typical automobile of the time had 15,000 parts. A B-17 had over a million. (OWI)

A seemingly endless row of center wing sections on rolling jigs is next to a similar row of nose sections, and another row of fuselages. All will be mated together, along with outer wings and empennages to form completed C-47s. These subassemblies won't sit here for long. At its peak, the Long Beach plant produced a completed plane every hour. (OWI)

Typically, the structural components of WWII aircraft were made of aluminum alloy, which was stronger than pure aluminum. The skin was usually made of Alclad, which was aluminum alloy with a thin layer of pure aluminum (about 5% of the thickness) bonded to the sheet, which gave it greater corrosion  resistance. Workers had to take care to avoid scratching this outer layer. (OWI)

Early aircraft were built with a robust frame to provide the necessary strength for the craft, because engineers were not able to calculate the strength provided by the skin. As the science of aeronautics progressed, this changed, and by WWII, planes were made of monocoque and semi-monocoque construction, which relied on the skin for much of the airframe's strength. Such is the case in this B-17 bomber. (OWI)

The trusswork of the wing of this B-17 bomber is revealed in this view. The B-17 was renowned for its ability to take a beating in combat, be riddled with bullet holes and have many parts carried away, yet still manage to make it home. The structural engineering in evidence here had a lot to do with that. (OWI)

On the left, B-17 fuselages are carried along on this overhead conveyor assembly line. At the right are jigs for building fuselage sections. The fuselage halves are assembled from prefabricated parts. The plant interior is as bright as noon on a sunny day, but it could be midnight - there are no skylights and no windows in this blackout facility. (OWI)

This view shows off the overhead conveyor system, as well as the light playing off the excellent sheet metal work on the B-17 fuselages it carries. By the end of the war, bomber production was such that the Allies were sending as many as 1,000 bombers on missions over German territory in a single day. (OWI)

These dorsal fins rest on top of the B-17 fuselage forward of the vertical stabilizer. Circular holes are punched in the ribs to lighten the parts. They are also flanged in the process, which provides stiffness and strength in the other dimension. (OWI)

This riveting machine operator is joining sections of wing ribs which will reinforce inner wing assemblies for the B-17F. The "B" is the Army indication for "bomber," and the "F" indicates the variant. Design improvements and other changes to meet specific needs in the war led to the creation of 15 variants for the B-17 over the course of its production. This was typical for most successful aircraft types. (OWI)

This technician is fitting the bombsight mount in the nose of this B-17. The mount will carry the Norden bombsight, the world's deadliest. Norden votaries joked that it could hit a pickle barrel from 30,000 feet. However, in actual combat, a bomber in 1942, at 20,000 ft., had only a 1.2% chance of hitting within 100 ft. of its target. America had a solution: more bombers. (OWI)

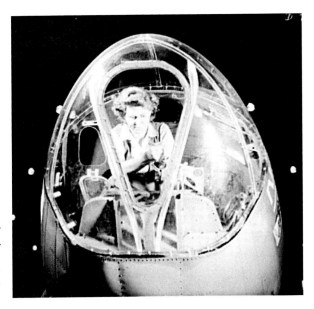

These assembly workers are drilling holes in a wing spar truss for a B-17. The heavy bomber's trusswork, though huge, must never-the-less be built to precise dimensions. Thus, the jig that holds it is built to close tolerances and checked often, and it utilizes a multitude of closely spaced clamps to hold the work in place securely. (OWI)

The Wright R-1820 Cyclone 9 engines on these rolling jigs will soon be mated with the B-17 wing sections being carried along on the overhead conveyor in the background. These nine-cylinder, air-cooled engines were used on the SBD Dauntless dive bomber as well as the B-17. (OWI)

Early in the production build-up, Donald Douglas wrote that "probably the greatest bottleneck is the lack of qualified machinists." Nothing could replace a machinist with decades of experience, but even though new employees might not have the knowledge to do the set-up on a machine tool, they quickly became productive as machine operators, as the quiet determination and confidence on this woman's face shows. (OWI)

The work on this spot-welding machine passes under the operator's feet as each weld is made. Aluminum is not as conducive to spot welding as steel is. However, when it was feasible to use spot welding, it had the advantage of being much faster than riveting, and it saved the weight of the rivets. This was not an unimportant consideration since even a medium-sized bomber contained 150,000 rivets. (OWI)

Douglas produced C-47 Skytrain transports, B-17 Flying Fortress bombers and A-20 Havoc attack bombers (pictured here in Oct. 1942) simultaneously in the sprawling Long Beach plant. Rather than one large building, the plant was built with 13 separate buildings, spaced out to minimize bomb damage should they be attacked. (OWI)

The Pratt & Whitney R-1830 engine is highlighted in this shot of a C-47. The 14-cylinder, radial engine (two rows of 7 cylinders) was used on some of the most successful planes (e.g., the C-47 and its civilian version, the DC-3, as well as the B-24 Liberator bomber). Pratt & Whitney built 173,618 of these engines, which is more than any other large aircraft engine in history. (OWI)

Thousands of ceiling lights are reflected in these Plexiglas noses for A-20 attack bombers. Despite its huge size the Long Beach plant brought in many parts and subassemblies made elsewhere, ranging from subcontractors across the country to Douglas's own plant in Santa Monica. The Long Beach facility had rail spurs to the various buildings and its own rail yard to sort and store cars of subassemblies and raw materials. (OWI)

A well-made plane with good wheel bearings can be pulled by hand, as this A-20 coming off the assembly line demonstrates. It will be transferred to the flight line and given a test flight before delivery to the Army. The agile A-20 helped  thwart Rommel in North Africa, and made history in the siege of Stalingrad. In gratitude, the Russians erected a statue of the A-20 in Moscow. (OWI)

These C-47s are packed cheek by jowl to the point where it looks as if it is a four-engine plane. It isn't. The ships do not yet have their outer wings, and the engine of one sits adjacent to that of the next ship. They have landing gear, but are supported by rolling jigs and move sideways down the line. The ship numbers on the noses were obliterated by censors. (OWI)

Even a manufacturing plant producing aircraft on the cutting edge of technology had need for the skills of a blacksmith. With his forge in the background, H. W. Helliker demonstrates his finesse with hammer and tong on hot steel in a Douglas smithy. (FP)

These feminine feet are building a Flying Fortress. The women are sitting on scaffolding while they work on the large wing of a B-17 Flying Fortress. Probably a greater proportion of the work on B-17s was done by women than any other plane. The well-scuffed shoes in this photo are reflection of the determination of these workers. The hand that rocked the cradle did a lot to rock the Axis back on its heels. (FP)

Hughes

Drilling for oil a century ago through Texas shale was not for the faint of heart. The flat fish-tail bits of the time were slow-cutting, and prone to catching and either breaking the bit or the drilling pipe. In 1909, Howard Hughes, Sr. patented the first roller cutter bit, which was less likely to break and cut 10 times faster than any previous bit. It revolutionized the industry.

In 1924, Howard Hughes, Sr. died, and ownership of the Hughes Tool Company passed to his 19-year-old son, Howard Hughes, Jr. The tool company's revenues enabled young Hughes to indulge in his passions, which ranged from movie-making to aircraft manufacturing.

Hughes Aircraft Company was initially a division of Hughes Tool. Beginning operations in a rented corner of a Lockheed Aircraft Corp. hangar in Burbank, it built the H-1 racer, which was the most advanced plane of its time. The sleek craft set a world airspeed record. Howard Hughes was awarded the annual prize for the world's most outstanding aviator. By 1939, he was fully engaged in an effort to develop the D-2, which was a high-speed fighter bomber.

Needing more room for this project, in July 1941, the firm opened a new facility in Culver City. There the company also built the H-4 Hercules transport (commonly called the "Spruce Goose"). Hughes got a development contract to build the huge wooden plane. The war ended, but Hughes completed the plane anyway.

Hughes Aircraft was also an active subcontractor in the war. It developed and patented a flexible feed chute for faster loading of machine guns on B-17 bombers, as well as manufactured electric booster drives for machine guns (which reduced the chance of jamming). Hughes produced more ammunition belts than any other American manufacturer, and built 5,576 wings and 6,370 rear fuselage sections for Vultee BT-13 trainers.

Hughes Aircraft grew after the war, and in 1953 Howard Hughes donated all of his stock in the company to the Howard Hughes Medical Institute. After Hughes died in 1976, the institute sold the company, which made it the second-best endowed medical research foundation in the world.

Howard Hughes (in the white shirt) is closely supervising the construction of the D-2 at the Hughes plant in Culver City in this ca. 1942 photo. Here he built the largest wooden building in the world, and next to it, the longest privately owned runway in the world (nearly two miles long). Here, he built the largest airplane in the world (and made it out of wood). (UNLV)

Hughes did not get a production contract for the D-2 fighter bomber, but out of the project emerged the XF-11 reconnaissance aircraft pictured here. Hughes was awarded a contract to build 100 of them for the Army, but the war ended, and only two prototypes were completed. (WMOF)

This XF-11 is at the Hughes plant with a Constellation, a notably successful plane developed by Lockheed for Trans World Airlines at the instigation of Howard Hughes, the major TWA stockholder. Hughes flew the first XF-11 prototype on its maiden flight.

An oil leak resulted in a propeller reversing pitch, and Hughes crashed while attempting to make an emergency landing at the Los Angeles Country Club, almost killing him. (MOF)

The H-4 Hercules flying boat (the "Spruce Goose") was conceived by Henry Kaiser, who built and operated shipyards producing Liberty Ships in the war. Mortified at the losses due to U-Boats, he proposed the plane as an unsinkable alternative to the Liberty Ship. Hughes and Kaiser teamed up and obtained a contract to build three prototypes, with the proviso that no strategic materials (e.g., aluminum) would be used. (MOF)

The massive 300,000-pound plane had a wing span of 320 feet. That was three times the wingspan of a C-47 transport or a B-17 bomber. It is even 50% greater than the wingspan of the largest modern 747s. Other aircraft manufacturers had their hands full with other projects and had no interest in attempting to build this wooden plane, which was widely considered to be impossible. (MOF)

Both the structure and surface of the plane were made of laminated wood. It was formed by steaming the wood plies, applying resin and putting them in special molds under heat and high pressure. The result was a rivet-free surface as smooth as glass. The public called the plane the "Spruce Goose," but it was actually made of birch. To this day, it remains the largest plane ever built. (WMOF)

The three prototypes were supposed to be built in 10 months, but after 16 months the first ship was barely under construction. The government cancelled the contract. Kaiser lost interest, but Hughes continued without Kaiser and obtained a new contract to build one plane. It was finally completed in 1946. Here it emerges from its Culver City hangar to embark on the 26-mile trip to Terminal Island. (WMOF)

The Hughes H-4 flying boat was transported in pieces on city streets by a house-moving company to Terminal Island. Shown here is the fuselage traveling across the Ocean Avenue pontoon bridge. This pontoon bridge was replaced by the Gerald Desmond Bridge in 1968. (MOF)

This view is looking eastward from Terminal Island toward Long Beach, with its many oil wells. A wing is on the pontoon bridge, towed by the house mover's truck piled high with timbers used as cribbing. Another wing follows closely behind. Moving the plane's sections from the Hughes plant in Culver City to the island took two days and necessitated moving or cutting 2,300 power and phone lines. (MOF)

This view of the H-4 flying boat assembly site on Terminal Island is looking northward. The Ocean Avenue pontoon bridge crossing the Long Beach main channel can be seen at the top right. Just out of view on the upper left was the yard of California Shipbuilding Corporation (Calship). From there it launched hundreds of Liberty Ships, whose sinkings prompted the building of the H-4. (WMOF)

The flying boat was assembled on the southeast corner of the island and a graving dock (an in-ground dry dock) was constructed just for it. The steam-powered, clam-shell crane is opening up a channel to be used by the plane when it is ready to taxi forth. The same will be done for the floats under each wing. (MOF)

Mechanics complete final work on the eight Pratt & Whitney R-4360-4A engines, each of which produces 3,000 h.p. The propellers are over 17 feet in diameter. The plane holds 14,000 gallons of fuel, enough to fill a small swimming pool. The unique plane still exists, preserved at the Evergreen Aviation & Space Museum in McMinnville, Oregon near Portland. (MOF)

The craft is nearly ready, with Howard Hughes, in his customary fedora hat, standing on top. Hughes engineers and craftsmen built an airplane that with only 24,000 horsepower, could lift itself with a loaded weight of 400,000 pounds, and then fly 3000 miles. This was a remarkable achievement for the 1940s. And they did it out of wood... (MOF)

Howard Hughes, standing, closely oversees the plane's preflight checkout, as he had its design and construction. When Henry Kaiser first came to him with the idea of building the huge flying boat, Hughes rebuffed him. Kaiser persisted, but his appeals fell on deaf ears. However, when Kaiser mentioned that other aircraft companies had told him it could not be done, Hughes's eyes brightened: "Oh, I don't know about that..." (WMOF)

Hughes, as pilot-in-command on the H-4, begins taxiing tests in Long Beach Harbor. Born in 1905, he had learned to fly at the age of 14. He set several speed and distance records, and won the Harmon Trophy, aviation's highest prize, twice. He had made movies, and courted Hollywood's leading ladies. Now he was about to see if this impossible-to-build aircraft would fly. (WMOF)

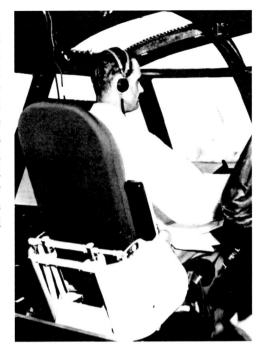

The H-4 taxied in Long Beach Harbor past the Rainbow Pier, which surrounded The Plunge bathhouse. Just to the west was The Pike amusement park. These landmarks are now gone, the area has been filled in, and the shoreline pushed southward. Above the bathhouse in the photo is The Breakers building, which still stands. On its cupola were two anti-aircraft gun installations. One of them is still there. (LBPL)

The day was supposed to be just taxi tests, and no flight plan had been filed. However, after taxing back and forth a few times, Hughes accelerated to 70 m.p.h. and lifted the plane into the air. It flew for a mile at 70 ft. altitude. The one-minute flight was its last. Having proved his point, Hughes put it in storage, where it remained until his death 30 years later. (WMOF)

Hughes had put his all into building the H-4, and he could have turned it over to the government, which owned it (and would have scrapped it). Instead, Hughes exercised an option in the agreement, and leased it for $450,000 per year. He built this hangar, paid rent to the port, and hired guards and mechanics to preserve it in airworthy condition. It cost him $1 million per year. (MOF)

Lockheed

Not every aviation pioneer with the intelligence of an engineer and the courage to be an entrepreneur became wealthy. The Loughead brothers are an example of this.

Allan Loughead (pronounced "Lockheed") and his brother, Malcolm, built their first airplane in 1913. The brothers engaged in various business ventures, most of them to build aircraft, but also a hydraulic brake business and even a tour-boat company on Catalina Island. They had a series of ups and downs, and went out of business several times.

Asked once if his Catalina business made any money, Alan Loughead laughed and responded, "No, we went broke, which was not a new experience!"

In 1916, they hired a young Jack Northrop as a draftsman. That firm went out of business in 1920, but by 1926, they were back in business making aircraft, with Northrop as chief engineer. This time their first product, the Vega, was a winner. The plane was built in the company's plant in Hollywood, trucked in pieces to Mines Field (today's LAX), and assembled there. The Vega was flown by legends such as Amelia Earhart, Charles Lindberg and Wiley Post. It was so popular that the firm moved to larger quarters in Burbank.

Jack Northrop left to start his own company in 1928, and the man they hired as his replacement was Gerald Vultee, who would also later found his own company, Vultee Aircraft.

Lockheed Aircraft (Tired of mispronunciations, the brothers spelled the business name phonetically) went broke in the Depression, but was bought by a group of investors in 1932. Alan Loughead was hired as a consultant, but no longer had an ownership interest.

The company succeeded, growing from only 4 employees in 1932 to 90,853 in 1943.

Lockheed built the P-38 Lightning fighter, which was one of the war's most distinctive and famous planes. It was designed by Lockheed's chief engineer, Clarence "Kelly" Johnson, who was one of the industry's most heralded designers. Johnson's boss, Hall Hibbard, once commented about his profound aeronautical engineering prowess, "That damned Swede can actually *see* air."

Lockheed had two large plants in Burbank in the war, one on the southeast side of the airport, and another a mile east, inside the "V" formed by the Southern Pacific (now Union Pacific) main lines. This eastward-looking view shows the latter. Along the railroad right of way is a long row of Lockheed Ventura bombers sans wings, resting on a piece of ground that was Lockheed's dirt airstrip in its early days. (SDASM)

The strength of this wing is being tested in the original Lockheed factory at 1006 N. Sycamore Street (and adjoining 1001 N. Orange Drive) in Hollywood in 1927. The company moved to Burbank the next year. It may be done now with a hydraulic ram instead of weights, but wings are still tested essentially the same way today. (WMOF)

In this section of the plant previously assembled sections were mated to form the P-38 Lightning fighter. On the left, behind the chain hoist, can be seen a center wing being joined to the ship's twin booms. More center wings, booms and main beams are to the right and in the background, awaiting their turn. Mating was a relatively quick operation – planes didn't stay here for long. (OWI)

The P-38 Lightning's twin engines gave it a speed of 400 mph, which was scarcely believable when it was introduced in 1941. It was one of the most feared planes of the war. America's top two aces of the war both flew P-38s. After encountering it over North Africa, the Luftwaffe pilots gave the P-38 the nickname *der Gabelschwanz Teufel,* the Fork-Tailed Devil. (HL)

Workers here are finishing a main beam for the center wing of a P-38. Once this subassembly is completed, it will be mated to the twin booms, then travel down the assembly line and gain engines, outer wings, landing gear and other equipment. (OWI)

An overhead crane is lowering this P-38 center section into a rolling jig. When Lockheed received the Army Air Corps' request for proposals for a fighter, the company had no previous military aircraft experience. Yet, the result was this revolutionary marvel, which destroyed more Japanese aircraft than any other plane. The P-38 was also the only American fighter to remain in production for the entire duration of the war. (OWI)

The assembly line ends here. The nearly complete P-38 is lifted off its cradle by the crane, the jig is rolled away, and the plane will ride on its own gear for the first time. Emerging through the plant's doors, it will feel the Southern California sun, have its propellers fitted, and then undergo trial flights. Lightnings served in all theaters of the war. (OWI)

This armorer and his assistant are checking the machine gun controls in the nose section of this P-38. Simulated firing was then conducted to ensure perfect operation of the control systems. Twin engines allowed all the armament to be clustered on the center nacelle, instead of wing-mounted guns firing criss-cross into a convergence zone. Thus pilots could shoot much further and straight ahead – a deadly advantage. (OWI)

Aircraft were inspected at every stage of production by Lockheed inspectors such as this one checking electrical assemblies. In addition to the countless manufacturer inspections, the Army and Navy had their own inspectors who checked aircraft during production. (OWI)

After some prodding by aircraft manufacturers, the government eventually learned that drafting employees with critical skills was not a good idea (Manufacturers asked: Do you want us to provide you with soldiers or airplanes?). Skilled employees such as this machinist were not only made exempt from the draft, but were even prohibited from enlisting. If they tried, the FBI would come get them and bring them back. (OWI)

This P-38 center section is held on edge in this jig to facilitate more efficient assembly. This 1942 photo shows a male workforce, which would soon change – 24,000 Lockheed employees entered the service. Women – often their wives or mothers - took their places. As the war progressed, young males in aircraft plant photographs were typically either those with critical skills or veterans who returned with missing arms or legs. (OWI)

This P-38 center section is being lifted by a chain hoist out of its fabrication jig and set into a mating jig to be joined with other subassemblies. The first US victory in combat against the Luftwaffe was won by a P-38. The Lightning was also the plane selected for the mission that shot down Admiral Isoroku Yamamoto's plane. (OWI)

Here a Lightning is lowered onto a rolling cradle to travel down the final assembly line, where it will receive wings, engines, landing gear and other equipment. The twin booms provided housing for the main landing gear when it was retracted and the General Electric turbochargers, as well as supported the twin fins and rudders. (OWI)

In 1944, Orville Wright, at the age of 72, took the controls of a Lockheed C-69 Constellation. It would be his last flight. The four-engine, pressurized-cabin "Connie" with a top speed of 340 mph (faster than a Japanese Zero), illustrated how far aeronautical engineering had come since the Wright brothers' first flight in 1903. His bright eyes and smile show that the delight of flight hasn't left him. (SDASM)

Riveter Mabel B. Cotton holds a Japanese flag sent to her by her son on Guadalcanal. Some females came to California aircraft plants hoping to get into Hollywood, and some came for the high pay that the jobs offered. For most though, patriotism was a factor, and many had family members in the service. To them, every rivet they set was a way of getting loved ones home quicker. (HL)

Wires were laid out and then harnessed together with string on these boards. The resulting bundles could then be installed quickly in the airplane on the assembly line. Mistakes could still be made, and more than once a delivery pilot would discover to her dismay that controls had been installed backwards. (HL)

P-38s are crowded outside the plant as they receive final inspections and adjustments. During the war Lockheed and other manufacturers often resorted to the "sunshine assembly line" to complete planes that were unfinished due to lack of parts, or as a way of speeding up operations inside the plant. (OWI)

Not bothered by the smoking cutting fluid, this turret lathe operator pulls the handle to draw the hexagonal turret (and thus the cutting tool) into the work. When William S. Knudsen, the president of General Motors, left to spearhead America's rearmament as director of the Office of Production Management, he knew what the first priority had to be: increase the production of machine tools. (HL)

With the hiring of women and others not used to working in an industrial environment, as well as the long work weeks of the war, came problems with extraordinarily high rates of turnover and absenteeism. Companies hired female matrons to counsel new employees, offered child care, and even provided lunchtime entertainment as a means of attracting and keeping employees. This company nurse seems to be enjoying the show. (HL)

One of the nice things about family visitors' day was that one might get to sit in a fire truck! (HL)

High-school students worked part-time, such as this youth who is using a type of pliers which apply/remove Cleco clips. These are temporary, spring-loaded fasteners, about the size of a spark plug, which hold sheet metal in place while it is being riveted. Riveting stretches the metal slightly, so without clips to hold it in position, after a few rivets were set, the holes would no longer line up. (HL)

This student is learning on some tools that are far older than she is. The drill press is a turn-of-the-century design. Instead of a chuck to hold the drill, the drill press utilizes a spindle with a tapered hole in it. The drill has a matching, precisely ground, smooth tapered shank, which fits into the hole, and stays there (without threads), defying gravity, simply because of the precise fit. (HL)

Hudson bombers make unusual deck cargo on this freighter (and perhaps prompted a few colorful conversations between the stevedore's superintendent and the ship's chief mate on how they should be stowed). Lockheed obtained an initial order from Britain's Royal Air Force for 250 planes and delivered them in 1939. The planes were "cocooned" to protect them from the elements. More will be loaded on the timbers laid out over the hatch cover. The outer wings have already been stowed below deck. The order was important to the RAF, but also for Lockheed. Without it, it may have gone bankrupt. (HL)

Shift change! This was the Lockheed plant (initially Vega, a Lockheed subsidiary) on N. Hollywood Way near Empire Avenue in Burbank. There aren't too many draft-age male faces left in this crowd. (HL)

This is the same area, but looking north instead of south. The plant is on the left. Notice the truss bridge of the Southern Pacific main line in the lower part of the photo (and in the background of the previous photo). On a span this large, the truss would have normally been made of steel, but because of wartime backlogs, it was made of wood. (HL)

The shear cuts sheet metal on the same principle as a paper cutter cuts paper. Some shears are hydraulic, and others mechanical, using a flywheel. The projecting arms support the work and also have T slots in them to hold adjustable stops that the operator can set at a measured distance from the blade. This enables him to cut multiple pieces to a consistent, precise size. (SDASM)

A planer can be used to put a flat, smooth surface (i.e., a plane) on a casting, or cut a groove. The work is secured to the table, and the whole table then travels back and forth under the cutting tool. The planer is useful for work on large  objects, as seen here, or many smaller objects can be attached to the table and all planed at once. (SDASM)

Lockheed (through its Vega subsidiary) built B-17 Flying Fortress bombers under license from Boeing, just as Douglas did. This four-engine heavy bomber was primarily employed in the daylight strategic bombing campaign against Germany. Useful against military and industrial targets, it was also used to a lesser extent against Japan. B-17s dropped more bombs than any other aircraft in World War II. (both HL)

This is a liquid-cooled Allison in-line engine being installed by Lockheed on a B-17 as a test. Concern that the Wright R-1820 radial engine, that was standard on the craft, might become scarce led to the experiment. They were discouraged by the fact that one of the Allison engines caught fire, and it was determined that they were more needed on other planes, such as the P-38 and P-51 fighters, so the project was terminated. (HL)

In June 1943, Lockheed installed a mechanized assembly line which more than doubled P-38 production. It was the first continuously moving assembly line for combat aircraft in the West. Shown here is a P-38 being lifted off its cradle jig at the end of the line and set onto its gear, after which it will roll out the plant door. (WMOF)

June 1943 - Before and After: The before photo (above) has only two lines, which were simply duplicates of one another, and the planes moved intermittently instead of continuously. In the after photo (below) a third line is now on the far right, where planes start at the back of the building (without wings, so that line was narrower). When they reach the end of that line, they shift to the center line, grow wings, and move backward down this line. Upon reaching the end, they are then shifted to the line at the left, and progress forward to the end of the line. The transition to this new system was accomplished in the amazingly short time of only 8 days, and during that period, P-38 production never stopped. It was continued outdoors. (above OWI, below AAF)

North American Aviation

Douglas Aircraft Company served as the incubator for not just Jack Northrop, president of Northrop Corporation, but also for James H. "Dutch" Kindelberger, who served as president of North American Aviation for three decades.

The son of German immigrants, Kindelberger, like Northrop, had a great engineering mind and the drive to run a business. When he was recruited from Douglas to run North American in 1934, North American had a grand total of one passenger aircraft on order.

Kindelberger successfully obtained a million-dollar order for BT-9 trainers. This evolved into the AT-6 Texan, the most universally used trainer ever built. It was used by both services (Army designation: AT-6. Navy designation: SNJ), as well as by the air forces of 30 allied nations.

To get orders for bombers, Kindelberger designed the XB-21. He lost out to the Douglas B-18A, but persisted and developed a more advanced design. This became the famous B-25 Mitchell bomber.

When Britain asked North American to build P-40 fighters, Kindelberger's response was that his company could design a better plane. Amazingly, in just 100 days from the time the designers first put their pencils to the drawing boards, the first P-51 Mustang was in the air.

The legendary Mustang is commonly rated as the greatest American fighter of the war, and by many as the most impressive fighter of all time.

Fitted with Rolls-Royce Merlin engines, later variants of Mustangs combined speeds of up to 487 mph with a range that would allow them to accompany bombers all the way into the heart of Germany. As Hermann Goering, the head of the Luftwaffe, observed, "When I saw Mustangs over Berlin, I knew it was all over."

North American was the largest producer of aircraft in the war by far. It was the first time a company had produced trainers, bombers and fighters simultaneously. And, the trainer North American produced (the AT-6/SNJ Texan) was the most important trainer, its bomber (the B-25 Mitchell) was the most important medium bomber, and its fighter (the P-51 Mustang) was the most important fighter.

This is the final assembly line for the B-25 Mitchell bomber. The two parallel lines of ships advance toward the camera on a mechanized track which moves intermittently. In the background is the white structure of the overhead-conveyor assembly line which is building fuselage and center-wing sections. (OWI)

In this view from to the opposite side, the trolleys and other details of the overhead-conveyor system can be seen in the foreground. To increase production, much work was purchased. By the end of 1941, North American was already using 65 major subcontractors, and 900 suppliers of parts and materials. Many stamped parts for the B-25 were made by Fisher Body Division of General Motors (in six different plants). (OWI)

One of the first things that long-time North American president James H. "Dutch" Kindelberger did when he took over in 1934 was to move the company from Maryland to Southern California to take advantage of the weather. This proved particularly advantageous during the massive production of the war. All the southland aircraft manufacturers found themselves doing at least some work outdoors, such as painting, installing parts that were late being produced, and doing production work while assembly lines were reconfigured. However, North American even went so far as to send B-25 bombers off the production line and out of the plant without their outer wings, as can be seen in the above photo. This saved production line width and made possible the two parallel final assembly lines. The outer wings were installed on the "sunshine production line," outdoors. (OWI)

In 1941 North American Aviation suffered a strike. Though a friend of labor unions, Franklin D. Roosevelt declared that he would seize the plant if the strike were not called off. That same day, picketers clashed with police. FDR ordered in the Army. Soldiers - with bayonets fixed - ensured the safety of those wishing to work. Public opinion turned against the union and the strike collapsed. (FP)

This man is operating a chain hoist attached to an electric trolley, which he is using to ease this Wright radial engine onto the firewall of a B-25. These supercharged, air-cooled engines had 14 cylinders (in two banks of seven). Each engine had a displacement of 2,600 cubic inches, weighed over 2,000 pounds, and produced 1,700 horsepower. (OWI)

Landing gear castings for the P-51 Mustang fighter are being machined on this milling machine. The mill (cutter) spins, but otherwise is stationary, and the table moves, carrying the work to it. Aluminum cuttings were carefully saved and sold to scrap yards for reuse. Rivets that were swept up off assembly line floors were not scrapped. They were sorted, by size, shape and composition, and reused. (OWI)

This woman is operating a turret lathe under the watchful eye of a seasoned machinist. She may not be able to gain all the accumulated knowledge that is in his head in the short time available, but she will learn a lot, and she will do her job well. This scene is emblematic of what was occurring in thousands of manufacturing plants across the country. (OWI)

Many jigs were made to great precision, and this skilled jig builder is using a surface plate and height gage to scribe a line on a metal plate prior to cutting it to the proper contour. Surface plates were made of cast iron (and later of granite), and ground and lapped to an extremely high degree of smoothness and flatness (e.g., ± .0001 in.). (OWI)

Templates were used in myriad applications to produce repeatable, accurate work, and do it quickly. Here, a steel template has been clamped to a stack of sheets of aluminum, and then this router is used to produce a dozen duplicates in a matter of minutes. (OWI)

The Industrial Revolution has produced the longest period of sustained growth in human history. This was achieved through the profit motive and the mass production of interchangeable parts. In World War II even items as large as airplane wings were  produced with the high degree of precision required to make them interchangeable. These B-25 wings are on rolling jigs and will soon join the main assembly line. (OWI)

This large press brake can quickly produce sheet-metal shapes such as flanges, channel or corrugations for aircraft structural parts such as stringers, stiffeners and longerons. Long pieces of flat stock are first set on the die. The moveable beam then descends, bringing a matching punch down onto the die, bending the work into the desired shape. (OWI)

Band saws are capable of cutting intricate curves on large pieces of steel or aluminum. Under the sheet metal being cut is a piece of plywood to support it on the ball table. As many as 100 sheets of metal can be stacked and clamped or screwed together, and all sawn at once. (OWI)

This seasoned employee is punching holes in sheet metal with a hand press. A multitude of punches are carried on the round carrousel, which can be revolved to place the one of desired size under the ram. (OWI)

One item that can be cut on a band saw is a wooden wheel… When suppliers ran behind, aircraft companies improvised. Rather than shut the production line down for lack of parts, planes were shoved out the door, and parked awaiting the needed parts. Temporary wooden wheels enabled P-51 Mustang fighters to be put onto their own gear and rolled off the end of the line onto the tarmac. Apparently someone at North American had a sense of humor. Scrawled on the side of the wooden wheel are the words "Do Not Inflate." (OWI)

Many aircraft parts, such as those in the foreground, were formed by a deep-draw operation on a drop hammer. The operator could control the speed of the hammer drop by snubbing the ropes. It took considerable skill on his part

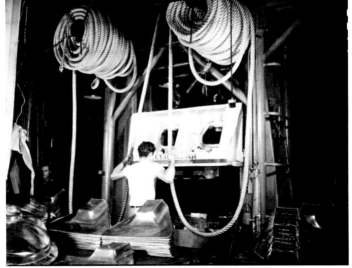

to avoid tearing the metal or creating wrinkles. The rope would wear on the revolving drum on which it rode, so spare rope was stored overhead on large coils. (OWI)

Female drop-hammer dies were made of Kirksite, a zinc alloy. They did not last as long as the tool-steel dies used in the automotive industry, but they were adequate for stamping aluminum, and they were much cheaper and quicker to make. The male dies were made of lead, and could be produced by pouring molten lead directly into the female die. The shrinkage when it hardened allowed for the thickness of the work. (OWI)

Making dies began with a plaster model, around which the Kirksite would be poured. Making these models required the skills of a sculptor and plaster mixed to the proper consistency. Aircraft plants often had separate buildings full of drop hammers to isolate their noise and vibration from the other operations. Drop hammers were often installed with their own individual foundations to absorb and isolate the impact. (OWI)

The tensile strength of aluminum alloys could be more than doubled by heat treatment. Aluminum could also be annealed to remove the hardness and strains that come from stamping operations. These men are putting these parts into an oven after they have been formed on a hydraulic press. (OWI)

The hydraulic press (commonly called a hydro press) was used for similar operations as the drop hammer. It was larger and more expensive, but was able to stamp out multiple parts with one stroke. By utilizing a team of employees, work could be fed and removed from the press quickly, greatly improving the productivity of the machine. (OWI)

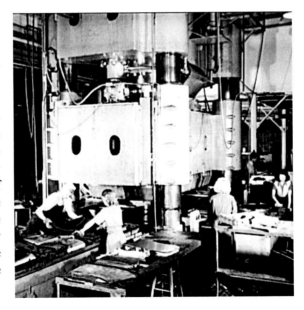

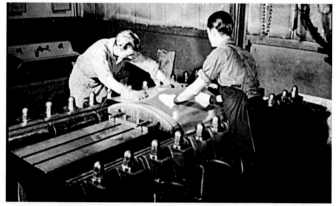

Sheet metal was formed by stretching on this machine. The edges of the sheet were clamped down, and the die below slowly raised using hydraulic power. Dies could be made of castings of zinc, lead or iron, or of wood or Masonite. Stretching machines were used to form cowling, wing tips, wheel fairings and other parts that were not highly stressed. (OWI)

Members of the engineering staff are observing tests on an accurate scale model of the B-25 in North American's redwood wind tunnel. The model's supports go through the floor, without touching it, and connect to scales which measure airflow forces on the plane, including lift, drag, side force, pitching, rolling and yaw. Graph paper moving through the recorders registers the results, enabling the analysis of different design options. (OWI)

Some planes were flown away, but others were shipped, particularly when sent to allies overseas early in the war years. Part of the aeronautical engineer's challenge is the practical consideration of how to fit an airplane into as small a crate as possible and protect it from damage. Shown here is an NA-57 trainer that will travel by rail to New Orleans, then by ship to France. (WMOF)

This skilled metal worker is using a tool called an English wheel to smooth imperfections on this cowling which has just been made on the hydro press. The rolling wheel above the cowling has a flat cross section. Hidden below the cowling is another wheel, called the anvil wheel, which has a slightly convex face. English wheels can be used to form remarkably intricate compound curves in sheet metal. (OWI)

The enormous power of the Rolls-Royce Merlin engine on this P-51 is palpable in this photograph. The P-51 epitomized the partnership between England and the United States. Putting this magnificent British-designed engine into the brilliantly designed American P-51 airframe produced the greatest fighter of the war. Many consider it to be the greatest fighter of all time. (MOF)

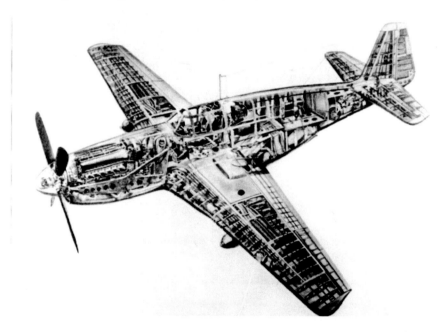

This cutaway drawing provides a view of what is under the skin of a P-51 Mustang. Wings hold fuel tanks, landing gear, machine guns and their long ammunition belts. Mustangs had a large fuel capacity to begin with, but by squeezing in another fuel tank behind the pilot (which was done on later variants), the plane was able to escort bombers all the way to Berlin. (WMOF)

Starting with the P-51D variant, Mustangs were built with a bubble canopy, which afforded the pilot 360-degree visibility. Shown here is a P-51H, the last variant of the Mustangs, which has benefited from countless engineering experiments and improvements. It represents the culmination of propeller-driven technology. This masterpiece is being put through its paces over Puddingstone Reservoir in San Dimas. (WMOF)

This herd of Mustangs is so large that it is spilling onto the dirt, yet this is only a few days worth of production. The camouflage of the North American plant is visible through the mist on the right. The P-51's tremendous speed (well over 400 mph for most variants) was partially due to the phenomenal Merlin engine, but also because of its remarkably low drag. (FP)

At this station on the production line the engine cowling is added, as well as control rods. These Wright R-2600-92 radial engines are air-cooled and have 14 cylinders producing 1,700 horsepower. They will be hung on North American's B-25 Mitchell bombers. (OWI)

This freshly minted Mustang is an experimental lightweight version (XP-51G) posing behind the North American plant as a southbound freight train passes by on the Santa Fe Railway's main line to the harbor. Mustangs had a laminar-flow wing, with a nearly flat profile and the high point further back on the wing than was customary. This smoothed air flow, thus reducing drag and contributing to the plane's exceptional performance. (FP)

Northrop

"Without question, Jack Northrop was the most talented, and at the same time, the most sincere and gracious person I have ever met." That's a rather nice thing to say. And, that is what Richard W. Millar, the president of Vultee Aircraft, and later, chairman of the board of Northrop, said of Jack Northrop.

The brilliant Theodore von Karman, a founder of the Jet Propulsion Laboratory, agreed, "Northrop was always one idea ahead of everyone else … a gentle, generous, and talented man with great daring."

Northrop Corporation reflected that. Actually, all three Northrop Corporations. Jack Northrop's first company foundered in the Depression. His second was dissolved due to labor problems. His third, founded in 1939, became one of the largest aircraft manufacturers in the country.

Northrop was a major subcontractor in the war, building subassemblies for Consolidated Aircraft's PBY flying boats and Boeing's B-17 Flying Fortress bombers. And, when Vultee Aircraft was packed with orders, Northrop took on a contract to build Vultee Vengeance dive bombers.

Northrop was a creative innovator from its earliest days, conducting extensive experimental work and building planes of its own design. Its P-61 Black Widow fighter was the first aircraft with design-integrated radar and designed specifically for night interception of enemy aircraft.

A flying wing is the most aerodynamically efficient design possible – the perfect airplane. Jack Northrop was intrigued by this concept from his earliest days as an engineer, and his firm built the first test model in 1940.

Additional prototypes were constructed, but the government ended the program after the war, which broke Jack Northrop's heart. The idea remained in mothballs for many decades until it was revived in the effort to create a stealth bomber.

Today's B-2 stealth bomber is the result. It was developed as a "black project" entailing the highest levels of secrecy.

Ronald Reagan signed off on special clearance to allow the elderly Jack Northrop to come see it under development. With his eyes becoming moist, a visibly moved Northrop reportedly expressed, "Now I know why God has kept me alive for the last 25 years."

The sheet-metal worker's art is evident from the light reflected off the smooth surfaces of these P-61 Black Widow night fighters on the final assembly line at Northrop. Center wings and fuselages take shape on left, with more nearly complete ships on the right. (AAF)

This P-61 is on a test flight over Palos Verdes in this view looking north. This innovative plane was built to carry the era's new radar units, which were heavy. This is one of the reasons it had two engines and was unusually large for a fighter. Its black paint indicates its mission – to fight at night. (NG, WMOF)

The Northrop plant was just south (to the right in the photo) of Northrop Field (present-day Hawthorne Airport). The building still exists, and is still in use as an aircraft plant. Now operated by Vought Aircraft Division of Triumph Aerostructures, the plant makes components for Boeing 787s and fuselage panels for 747s. The panels are shipped in specially designed rail cars to the Boeing plant in Washington. (NG, WMOF)

This is the P-61 final assembly line looking northward in the plant. P-61 engines had a water-injection system that would cool the combustion chambers, allowing for greater compression ratios, thus effectively increasing the octane rating of the fuel. This could be used for short bursts of speed under W.E.P. (War Emergency Power) by the pilot by pushing the throttle past its normal full-throttle position. (NG, WMOF)

This 1927 or early 1928 photo shows a young Jack Northrop, working for Lockheed then with this team that created the famous Vega. At the top are Anthony Stadlman (left) factory superintendent, and Ben Hunter (right), executive vice president. Gerard Vultee, designer, is inside the Vega fuselage. In front are Jack Northrop (left), chief engineer, W. Kenneth Jay (center) secretary/treasurer, and Allan Loughead (right), vice president and general manager. (SDASM)

These workers grouped around a P-61 nose give just a hint of what a large fighter it was. It was built large enough to carry fuel to fly for at least eight hours, during which time it could do a lot of damage. Later variants were equipped with 20-mm cannons, which proved highly effective in destroying large numbers of German locomotives and military convoys in the Battle of the Bulge. (NG, WMOF)

Revealed here is the night fighter's radar unit inside the nose. British research begun in 1936 led to the invention of the ground-based radar units which enabled the vastly outnumbered Royal Air Force to successfully defend England in the Battle of Britain. Realizing how valuable it would be to have radar in the aircraft itself, it was the British who then prompted Northrop to develop the P-61. (AAF)

One of the P-61's many design features that was a military secret was its retractable ailerons. They rested in slots and could be raised by the pilot as needed in making turns. This feature allowed for the use of full-span wing flaps, thus increasing braking power. This enabled the plane to land on "postage stamp" airstrips, even in heavy fog or in the dead of night. (NG, WMOF)

In December 1942, Northrop was the first war production plant to sponsor a family visiting day. It was immensely popular – the *Los Angeles Times* estimated 35-40,000 visitors. These well-dressed family members are viewing Northrop's production line for V-72 Vengeance dive bombers (built under license from Vultee), under the watchful eye of the Military Police. (NG, WMOF)

The popularity of family visiting day spread to other aircraft manufacturers and Northrop repeated it again in future years. Being built here are Vengeance dive bombers, which had the unique feature that the wing's angle of incidence was *zero* degrees (the degree of tilt of the wing in relation to the fuselage). This enabled the plane to dive straight down on its target. (NG, WMOF)

Air-cooled radial engines (left) and a water-cooled in-line engine (front right), each had their advantages. Air-cooled engines did not have the weight of a water cooling system or its vulnerability to enemy fire. In-line engines presented less  frontal area and thus less drag. Maj. Gen. George H. Brett, chief of the Army Air Corps, studied the matter. His conclusion? Build both … as fast as you can. (NG, WMOF)

Master templates were made to great precision, often to ±.001 inch. From these, lighter-gage shop templates would be made, typically of 1/8-inch steel. George Phillips is on the left cutting and Carl Goedecke is on the right front filing templates. Templates were used as layout guides, drill guides, trimming guides, and for checking contours. A typical aircraft plant employed templates that numbered in the thousands. (NG, WMOF)

When Northrop Corporation began in 1939 it started off doing subcontract work making PBY flying boat subassemblies for Consolidated Aircraft in San Diego. However, Northrop almost immediately began designing and building its own aircraft, the first of which was also a seaplane, the N-3PB patrol bomber. The plane was first test flown on November 1, 1940 at Lake Elsinore. (NG, WMOF)

After being trucked out there in pieces, the plane was assembled on the beach. The plane was ordered by the Norwegian government in March 12, 1940, but shortly thereafter Norway was invaded by Germany. The aircraft were produced anyway, and delivered to the Royal Norwegian Naval Air Force, which operated as a unit of the British RAF outside of Norway. The N-3PB was the world's fastest military sea plane. (NG)

This was the N-3PB assembly line. The simple, un-mechanized setup made economic sense for a short production run. Northrop built 24 of these planes for Norway. (NG)

The pacific waters of Lake Elsinore in these photos may be a bit calmer than the North Atlantic conditions the plane would eventually face. The first production N-3PBs rolled off the Northrop assembly line only eight months after the order was placed. They were used in training, on anti-submarine patrols and as convoy escorts. Based in Reykjavik, Iceland, the planes carried out attacks on eight German U-boats. (NG, WMOF)

The N-3PBs exceeded all performance estimates. After the war, though, all the surviving planes were scrapped. However, in 1979, one that had been wrecked in 1943 was pulled out of a river in Iceland. It was brought to Northrop in Hawthorne, and with the help of Northrop, Northrop retirees and volunteers from the Western Museum of Flight in Torrance, has been fully restored. (NG, WMOF)

An example of Northrop's inventive spirit is the XP-56, one of the most radical experimental planes built during WWII. It had no horizontal tail, only a small vertical tail, an experimental engine, and it was built out of magnesium. Magnesium, a metal not used in aircraft of the time, was used for both the airframe and the skin. Northrop even developed special techniques using heliarc welding for the project. (AAF)

Jack Northrop had been experimenting with the flying wing concept since 1928. In 1941, Northrop obtained a development order for a flying wing bomber prototype in 1/3 scale. Designated the N-9M, it was to be used to evaluate  flight performance. The central section was made of tubular steel, part of the framework was made of wood, and the skin was laminated wood plies. (NG, WMOF)

Between 1941 and 1944, there would be four flying wing prototypes built, the N-9M-1, N-9M-2, N-9M-A and N-9M-B. Originally, they were powered with Menasco C6S-1 inverted engines (with crankshaft on top, and spark plugs on the bottom). The in-line, air-cooled, six-cylinder, 290-h.p. engines drove twin-bladed propellers. (NG, WMOF)

The first N-9M made its first test flight on December 27, 1942, and made 45 test flights over the next five months. Most of the flights ended with mechanical problems, and on May 19, 1943, it crashed near Muroc Army Air Base (today's Edwards AFB), killing the pilot. (NG, WMOF)

The N-9M-B, pictured here, was upgraded with 400 h.p. Franklin engines and other steps were also taken to resolve various other mechanical problems. The planes presented numerous engineering challenges. These ranged from "buried" engine installations with their problems of mounting, cooling and driving through long shafts to remote propellers, to creating methods to effectively control the aircraft in flight. (NG, WMOF)

These N-9Ms are on a test flight at Muroc Army Air Base. The Corum family homesteaded here in 1910. Since there was already a town named Corum in California, the first post office was named Muroc (Corum spelled backwards). It was renamed Edwards Air Force Base, after pilot Glen Edwards, who was killed in 1948, along with five others, while testing a full-scale version of a flying wing. (NG, WMOF)

The flying wing, with its perfect aerodynamic shape, should be able to carry a payload faster, farther and cheaper than a conventional bomber. In 1941, the Army Air Corps was interested in this concept as a way of conducting long-range bombing of Nazi-occupied Europe if Britain fell. Work on the full-size XB-35, shown here, commenced in 1942, while testing with the N-9M models was still underway. (NG, WMOF)

To test the installation and operation of the XB-35 engines, Northrop built this test stand. It consisted of a full-scale section of the wing, including engine mounts. The recording instruments required over 12 miles of temperature-sensitive wiring and transmission tubing. At the time, it was the largest engine test stand in the world. (NG, MOF)

The Army ordered 13 YB-35s, seen here at the Northrop plant. The war ended and the engineering challenges continued. Jack Northrop said later that Secretary of the Air Force Stuart Symington urged him to merge with Convair on unfavorable terms (which Northrop refused). In 1950, Symington cancelled all flying wing contracts, and Convair received the bomber contracts. Shortly thereafter, Symington left his position and became president of Convair. (NG, MOF)

Vultee

Working at Jack Northrop's elbow in the engineering department at Douglas Aircraft Company in the 1920's was a young engineer named Gerard "Jerry" Vultee. Douglas was busy with military planes, and having ideas for commercial aircraft, Northrop went to Lockheed in 1927. The next year, he recruited Vultee to join him.

Northrop left Lockheed in 1928, and Jerry Vultee became chief engineer. Lockheed went bankrupt during the Depression, leaving Vultee out of a job, but he searched for financial backing for his ideas and found it in the form of E. L. Cord, head of Cord Corporation.

Working out of a hangar in Burbank, Vultee designed and built the V-1 transport, and obtained orders for 10 of the planes from American Airways. Within a few years, Vultee was operating out of a larger plant in Downey, supervising 1,500 employees, and had an order backlog of a million dollars.

In 1938, coming home after presenting a new aircraft to the Army in Washington, D.C., Jerry Vultee was killed when his plane crashed into a mountain near Sedona, Arizona in a snowstorm. He was 38 years old.

His company continued to grow, though, and by 1940, the plant had doubled in size. By 1941, Vultee was producing 15% of all military aircraft in the nation.

Vultee's most famous product was the ubiquitous BT-13 Valiant trainer ("BT" was the Army's designation for "Basic Trainer." The Navy version was the SNV). Almost every US pilot and many allied pilots learned their basic flying skills in this plane.

Vultee was the first to experiment with putting women to work in production positions. The company's masterpiece was the aircraft manufacturing industry's first powered assembly line.

Built in 1941 (before Pearl Harbor), this bold investment quadrupled the plant's production. Floor space was saved by placing all conveyor machinery overhead. The conveyor system was over a mile long (6,280 ft.), and included numerous feeder lines bringing parts to the main line at given points. Speed of the conveyors could be adjusted as needed. The firm's innovation resulted in a significant improvement in efficiency, including a 50% decrease in final assembly time alone.

Orange groves no longer border Bellflower Blvd., and Vultee has long since become part of Rockwell International, but part of the Vultee plant in Downey remains. At this writing, most of it is being redeveloped into a shopping mall, but some of the original buildings along Bellflower Blvd. will be saved and rented out as office space. (MOF)

Aeronautical engineers today seldom wear vests to work, or sit on stools, or work on drafting tables supported by sawhorses. In 1942 though, these men were accomplishing a lot with a 2H pencil, a triangle and a sheet of velum. (SDASM)

In 1941, Vultee installed the first powered assembly line in the industry. It also was the first to hire women for production positions, which it did before Pearl Harbor, wisely anticipating that it might lose male workers to the draft. These women are working on a BT-13 Valiant basic trainer, which is built around this sturdy tubular-steel frame. (OWI)

Vultee's 6,280-foot-long conveyor system included feeder lines bringing subassemblies, such as these BT-13 wings, into the oval-shaped fuselage line at various points. This system enabled Vultee to produce more planes in a shorter time span than any similar plant. (OWI)

For final assembly, the BT-13 trainers were moved along on this ground track – backwards. Outer wings were added - one first (as can be seen in the foreground), then the other, later in the line. Part of the fuselage overhead conveyor system loop can be seen at the left of the photograph. The line eliminated backtracking, and simplified tasks so that the thousands of new employees could be quickly trained. (OWI)

At each station, the once-bare steel frame looks more and more like an airplane. The fuselage line had 25 stations, after which the planes would be removed from their conveyor cradles, and roll on their own gear for final assembly. The BT-13 trainer used a lot of steel, which gave it the strength to withstand abuse from new pilots and also made aluminum available for combat aircraft. (OWI)

This view from the opposite end shows the nearly complete planes about to roll off the line into the California sun. As war approached, the need to train new pilots increased astronomically. In 1939, the Army Air Corps ordered 300 BT-13 trainers from Vultee, which  was the largest order it had ever placed. That would soon be exceeded... (OWI)

The vastness of the Vultee factory floor is evident in this view. Vultee built trainers for the Army, Navy and Marine Corps, as well as produced subassemblies for Consolidated Aircraft in San Diego. Vultee produced more trainers than all other manufacturers combined. (OWI)

Saving weight in a trainer was not critical, so use of costly and scarce aluminum was minimized. Frames were steel, and flaps and other control surfaces were made of fabric, sewn on by hand. The mercerized cotton was carefully cut so that the warp threads were parallel to the line of flight. It was painted with several coats of dope, which dried and shrank, strengthening and stiffening the surface. (OWI)

With one hand on the controls for the electric trolley for the chain hoist, and the other to guide the free-swinging powerplant, this man is hanging an engine on the firewall of this BT-13. The engine is a Model R-985-AN-1, an air-cooled, nine-cylinder, 450 h.p. radial engine made by Pratt & Whitney. The highly regarded engine was introduced in 1929, and P&W was still producing them into the 1950s. (OWI)

After being hung, the engine's myriad plumbing and electrical connections were made. The vast majority of American pilots learned to fly in a BT-13 basic trainer. Their initial contact with an airplane was a very simple primary trainer, then, if they hadn't washed out, they moved up to the basic trainer (the "BT" in BT-13). From there, they would progress to an advanced trainer. (OWI)

Little people had advantages that others didn't have working in the numerous confined spaces found in aircraft. Here, control cables are being installed on this BT-13. Rudders and other control surfaces on large bombers were operated by hydraulics. On smaller planes though, it was common for the pilot's stick and foot pedals to operate wire cables running through pulleys to operate the control surfaces. (OWI)

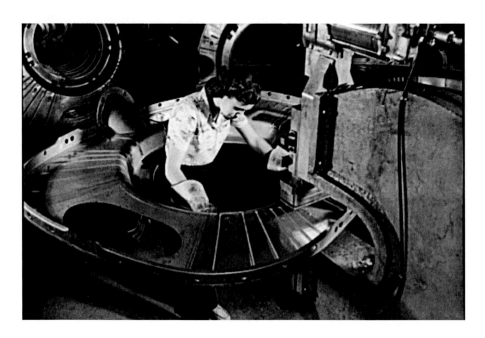

In 1941, Vultee purchased 34% of Consolidated Aircraft in San Diego. The two companies gradually became more interwoven, and Vultee merged with Consolidated in 1943. Vultee made subassemblies for Consolidated, such as these engine cowl rings being produced in 1942 for the B-24 bomber, which Consolidated built in San Diego. (OWI)

Vultee's busy, yet immaculate, machine shop boasts a gang of horizontal milling machines in the foreground, a shaper, and three healthy-looking engine lathes in the best-lit spot, next to the windows. The roof's north-facing clerestory windows were designed to bring in valuable light, but not direct sun. With the war, the windows would soon be painted over, the building camouflaged, and an anti-aircraft gun added to the roof. (SDASM)

Machine shops are only kept immaculate with regular attention paid to housekeeping. The size of the scrap pile here gives an indication of the volume of machine work done at Vultee. (OWI)

The Farnham Roll is used to put a radius on sheet metal, such as on the leading edge of wings, as seen here. The metal is fed between three rolls, and the distance between the rolls adjusted to produce the desired curvature. It can even produce a conical shape by setting one end of the rolls farther apart than the other. (OWI)

Wood was not just used in making models for wind tunnels. In trainers performance was not the primary consideration, so Vultee redesigned its BT-13 to use less aluminum. By 1943, the plane was 70% wood and plastics, saving enough aluminum to build 400 more of its Vengeance dive bombers annually. Whether making aircraft parts or providing support to an engineer's drafting table, wood and woodworkers had value. (OWI)

Some operations at Vultee were performed in stationary jigs before being fed to the moving assembly lines. The lightening holes in the wing's rib on the right save weight with almost no reduction in strength. As with a truss bridge, the greatest tension or compression forces are along the edges, not in the middle. The occasional solid section to keep the edges the proper distance apart is sufficient. (OWI)

For smaller subassemblies it was possible to utilize a riveting machine. This was faster and could be done without a bucker. The machine sets the rivets by squeezing them, rather than pounding them, so there is no distortion of the sheet metal. This provides another advantage: no Cleco clips are needed. (OWI)

This welder is performing oxy-acetylene welding on the steel exhaust system of a BT-13. Women at Vultee had a tendency to come in to work and look at the production of men on the previous shift, and then attempt to beat it. No wonder Vultee was happy to hire them. (OWI)

This man is operating a circular shear. The rotating blades of the compact machine work similarly to an electric can opener. It is not as fast as a large squaring shear, but, as seen here, it can cut virtually any curve, and do it on metal of virtually any contour. (OWI)

Most aluminum arrived at aircraft factories in the form of large sheets. Aluminum came in various alloys, and in designing an airplane, engineers would make their selection taking into consideration the properties of the different alloys, such as: ductility (the ability of the metal to be drawn without fracture), malleability (its ability to be hammered without cracking), elasticity, hardness, toughness, fatigue resistance, and strength. (OWI)

118

With the careful, coordinated efforts of four men, it was occasionally possible to cast a die without splattering too much molten zinc on one's pants... (SDASM)

These riveters and their buckers are building fuselage sections for BT-13 trainers. The jig designer's challenge was to not only create a jig that would hold parts into the precise position needed for assembly, but also to mount the many odd shapes into positions in which they could be worked on without too much difficulty. These subassemblies will soon be out of these jigs and moved to the assembly line. (OWI)

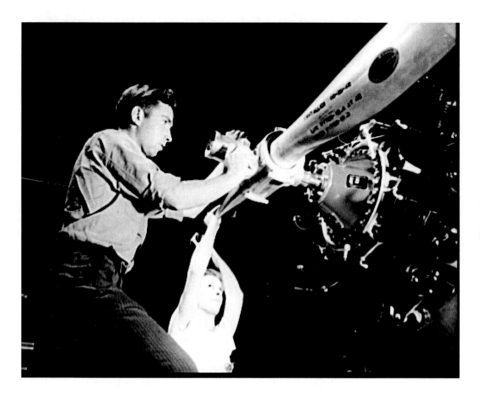

The hub is being installed on the end of the crankshaft to hold this variable-pitch Hamilton propeller onto the Pratt & Whitney Wasp radial engine of this BT-13A Valliant basic trainer. The variable pitch propeller adjusts for different thrust levels and air speeds, which allows the engine to operate in its most economical range of rotational speeds. (OWI)

After casting dies, a little grinding is done with the air-powered grinder to smooth out the surface. Sitting on the bench in the foreground is another grinder designed to get into smaller spaces with concave curves. (SDASM)

Other Manufacturers and Subcontractors

Not only was the Los Angeles area the headquarters for six major aircraft manufacturers, it was also home to numerous smaller airframe manufacturers and even to three companies that made aircraft engines.

The term "subcontractor" was unused in the industry until World War II. Prior to that time, aircraft manufacturers had small orders and made virtually the entire plane themselves. The war quickly changed this.

Convair in San Diego, for example, by 1943 had nearly 100 subcontractors sending it subassemblies, including large items such as horizontal and vertical stabilizers, and bomb-bay doors. Convair also established a network of 11 feeder plants, centered 100 miles north in Orange County, where labor was available.

Some of the smaller aircraft manufacturers in the Los Angeles area were small businesses that made a prototype or two, hoping to land a production contract, but were not successful. Other small companies, though, made hundreds of planes and were active as subcontractors.

The list of names is surprisingly long and includes: Doak Aircraft in Torrance, Fletcher Aviation in Pasadena, Harlow Aircraft in Alhambra, Interstate Aviation & Engineering in El Segundo, Manta Aircraft in Los Angeles, Phillips Aviation in Los Angeles, and Timm Aircraft in Van Nuys.

Some of these were aviation pioneers, such as Doak. As a young man, Edmond Doak worked for both Donald Douglas and North American Aviation, and then, as the war approached, he founded his own company in Hermosa Beach, and later at 2321 Abalone St., in Torrance. Doak Aircraft produced 1,000 fuselage sections for the Vultee BT-13 and North American AT-6, as well as doors, hatches and gun turrets for nearly every aircraft manufacturer. Doak designed and produced its own trainer, but did not land a production contract. After the war, Doak went on to design and build one of the first VTOL planes (with tiltable propellers, enabling it to take off or land vertically).

This is just one example of the many smaller local firms engaged in aircraft work. In addition to those building planes and engines, there were countless machine shops and others applying their industrial might to defeat totalitarianism.

Menasco Mfg. Co. manufactured aircraft engines in this plant at 805 S. San Fernando Road, Burbank. Its original factory was at 6917 McKinley Ave., Los Angeles, which it continued to use as its foundry when it opened the Burbank facility. Menasco made not only thousands of aircraft engines, but also manufactured landing gear for the P-38 Lightning, being built at the Lockheed plant a few blocks away. Albert S. (Al) Menasco designed and built engines with an interesting design feature – they were upside down. The crankshaft was on top and the sparkplugs on the bottom. This design not only allowed improved ground clearance for the propeller, but also better visibility for the pilot. (SDASM)

This prewar view of Menasco's shop shows modern machine tools in the foreground drawing electricity through new conduit coming down from above. In the background, an overhead line shaft with pulleys turns wide flat belts to operate the machines below. This method goes back to pre-electricity days when a single steam engine would be used to power the line shaft, which then drove all the machines. (van Rossem photo, WMOF)

This photo of Menasco's machine shop shows how an engine's crankshaft is turned on a lathe. After the crankshaft is forged, each journal is lined up and turned individually. The holes inside the journal sections are to lighten the part - a feature of aircraft engines, but not worth the expense on land or marine engines. (SDASM)

A turret lathe, such as this one at Menasco, typically has a turret with six faces, each of which can hold a separate cutting tool. Thus, multiple operations can be carried out on a part without the time involved to make a new set-up. This intent machinist has successfully stayed out of the way of the cutting fluid which is continuously lubricating the bit, and splattering around the machine. (SDASM)

These well-lubricated Menasco mechanics are adding oil or some other fluid to this nine-cylinder radial engine being put through its paces on a test stand, as the technician inside the test booth looks on. Four-stroke radial engines always have an odd number of cylinders. This enables a firing order of every other cylinder. Just visible through the door is the company's rail spur. The photo below shows the inside of the test booth. (WMOF and SDASM)

Interstate Aviation & Engineering Corp., 2600 W. Imperial Hwy., El Segundo, built 250 of these liaison/observation planes for the Army. It also built trainers and made parts for other airframe manufacturers, such as bomb shackles and machine gun chargers. The windows of this observation plane cant outward enabling the observer to see directly below the plane. It was also designed to allow him to use a collapsible drawing table. (MOF)

In 1915, barnstormer Otto Timm crashed his plane in Bert Kinner's field in Minnesota on a cross-country trip. Kinner repaired the engine for Timm and was fascinated. Both came to California, and started aircraft manufacturing businesses in Glendale. Shown here is a Timm Collegiate, sporting a Kinner engine. Timm built planes for both the Navy and Army, and Kinner became the West Coast's largest producer of aircraft engines in 1941. (MOF)

Timm began at 901 N. San Fernando Road in Glendale, and later moved to Metropolitan Airport in Van Nuys. In 1941, he secured a Navy order for 260 trainers. His profits increased to $70,000, up from $240 the previous year... In 1942, Timm built 434 CG-4 assault gliders, shown above, under license from Waco Aircraft Company. The most widely used gliders of the war, they landed troops on D-Day. (AAF)

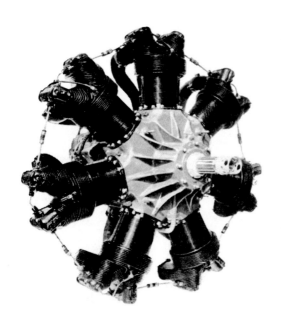

Bert Kinner designed and built the K-1 Airster, which was the first airplane that Amelia Earhart owned. He also designed and built four other models of aircraft, as well as four models of radial engines, ranging from 100 h.p. to 350 h.p. (The latter is shown here). During the war Kinner produced thousands of engines that were used in trainer aircraft. (AAF)

One of the countless machine shops doing work for the war effort was Parker Manufacturing Company in Santa Monica. The company's order books were full, and its building full of lathes, milling machines, presses, shaper, planer, and other machine tools was busy. Among other things, it produced parts for aircraft wings, tools and dies, and precision fuses for bombs. (PMC)

Shortly after the war, Parker needed a shear, but it would be a two-year wait since machine-tool manufacturers still had heavy backlogs. So, the company made its own shear. Foundries were backlogged, so they made it entirely out of steel plate – no castings. Others saw it and wanted it. Soon the company was in the shear manufacturing business. This unique shear exemplifies the ingenuity prompted by the war. (PMC)

Max Harlow, a professor at Pasadena Jr. College, oversaw the design and construction of an airplane as a class project. In 1936, he founded Harlow Aircraft Company to build a production version of the craft in a plant at Alhambra Airport. The Harlow PC-5, above, was a military training version. The Army Air Corps did not place an order, but the planes were exported to India. (MOF)

Jack Northrop wasn't the only one interested in the flying-wing concept. William H. Bowlus, a sailplane and glider manufacturer in Los Angeles, designed a flying wing in 1942, seen here flying over Oxnard. The glider's front wing opened up like a large mouth to accept cargo. On its test flight from March Field in 1943, it crashed, killing several dignitaries who were passengers. The project was cancelled in 1944. (AAF)

Reginald Denny was a well-known actor of the era, performing in over 200 stage shows and movies. Less known is the fact that he was the "Father of the Target Drone." His Radioplane Company at Metropolitan Airport (present-day Van Nuys Airport) built radio-controlled target drones for the Army Air Forces and the Navy during the war. (NG, WMOF)

The Radioplane plant shows that small companies, even without an automated conveyor system, could produce their products with a rather sophisticated layout. A waist-height assembly line, with hinge-down ramps between tables, and strategically placed parts carts testify to this well-thought-out plant. Radioplane made thousands of drones during the war, and by 1945 could produce 40 per day. (NG, WMOF)

Denny and his partners had a number of early learning experiences (i.e., failures) when testing their first experimental radio-controlled planes. Tired of seeing their hard work destroyed in disheartening crashes, they sought a better way to see how the plane responded to radio commands. Perhaps a sturdy Packard and a trip to a dry lake bed in the Mojave Desert would serve the purpose… (NG, WMOF)

The drones even had parachutes to minimize damage after being shot down. One of the employees packing those parachutes was the young wife of a merchant seaman. After being photographed displaying the company's products, Norma Jean Dougherty was advised to apply for a job at a modeling agency. Soon, her hair color would change from brown to blond, and her name would change also, to Marilyn Monroe. (USA)

Epilogue

The English language may run short of adjectives powerful enough to describe the manufacturing achievement of World War II, but a few statistics can sum it up.

In 1933, all the aircraft factories in Southern California combined employed a grand total of about 1,000 people. By November 1943, that number had grown to 230,000 workers.

By the end of WWII, fully half of all of the world's industrial production took place in the United States.

As the war drew to an end, most economists and New Deal policy makers assumed that without the massive government spending of the war, the pre-war Great Depression and its huge unemployment would return. The prevailing Keynesian economic wisdom predicted economic disaster when the war ended.

One of the leading businessmen of the day (and one of the New Dealers' favorite targets) was Alfred P. Sloan, president of General Motors. He disagreed with the economists.

Instead of the predicted return of the Depression, he predicted a post-war boom.

He was right.

After the war, the government cancelled military contracts outright. Orders for thousands of planes and all of the other implements of war were abruptly terminated. Whole plants were closed.

In addition, men were mustered out of the service by the millions.

Government spending was drastically cut back.

However, instead of a return to the Great Depression, one of the greatest periods of economic expansion in American history resulted. The women and others who had flocked to war-plant jobs knew that the jobs would only be "for the duration." They saved much of their paychecks. Now many of them married returning soldiers, and bought homes, cars, and refrigerators. Just as business had reacted quickly to the demand for war goods, now it reacted just as quickly to produce consumer goods. A period of prosperity that lasted for decades ensued.

Southern California's aircraft industry transitioned into aerospace. Of the country's 25 largest aerospace companies, 15 of them were headquartered here. Putting a man on the moon was just as much an accomplishment of Southern Californians as it was of those in Cape Kennedy or Houston.

In the past couple of decades though, the California economy and business climate has lost much of its luster, and this has been particularly true in aerospace. In the 1990's alone Southern California aerospace employment dropped by over 50%. Many companies have shifted work to states with lower tax burdens, faster permitting processes, and less onerous regulatory environments.

Business executives have also pointed out that California high schools and colleges are not producing enough graduates with "STEM" skills - science, technology, engineering and mathematics. One medium-sized aerospace business owner called for a return to shop classes in high schools, saying that he was unable to bid on jobs due a lack of welders.

However, not all of the industry is gone. California still employs more aerospace workers than any other state. Major components for the Boeing 747 and 787 are produced in Hawthorne and the Inland Empire. Northrop Grumman builds approximately 40% of the F/A-18, and fuselages for the F-35 Joint Strike Fighter, as well as Global Hawk drones in Southern California plants. A major supplier of aircraft fasteners is based in Carson, and Predator drones are built near San Diego. Sea Launch puts satellites into orbit from rockets launched from ships based in Long Beach. Space Exploration Technologies (SpaceX), based in El Segundo, is a private firm building space vehicles to launch satellites and play other roles similar to those formerly performed by the Space Shuttle.

Not all of California's aerospace manufacturing is in the past...

Sources

Aero Digest magazine, 1940-1945. Aeronautical Digest Publishing Corp.

Aviation magazine, 1940-1945. McGraw-Hill Publishing Co., Inc.

Borth, Christy. *Masters of Mass Production.* Bobbs-Merrill Co., 1945.

Douglas Aircraft Company, *The Airview* magazine, 1940-1945.

Herman, Arthur. *Freedom's Forge: How American Business Produced Victory in World War II.* Random House, 2012.

Los Angeles Times, 1940-1945

Mingos, Howard, editor. *The Aircraft Year Book for 1940-1945.* Aeronautical Chamber of Commerce of America, Inc.

North American Aviation. *North American Skyline* magazine, 1940-1945.

O'Leary, Michael. *Building the P-51 Mustang.* Specialty Press, 2010.

Overy, Richard. *Why the Allies Won.* W. W. Norton & Co., 1995.

Rae, John B. *Climb to Greatness: The American Aircraft Industry, 1920-1960.* The MIT Press, 1968.

Reid, Constance Bowman. *Slacks & Calluses: Our Summer in a Bomber Factory.* Longmans, Green & Co., 1944. Smithsonian Institution, 1999.

Stoff, Joshua. *Picture History of World War II American Aircraft Production.* Dover Publications, Inc., 1993.

Western Flying magazine, 1940-1945. Occidental Publishing Co.

Wrynn, V. Dennis. *Forge of Freedom: American Aircraft Production in World War II.* Motorbooks International, 1995.

Yeakley, James R. *Aircraft Tooling Practices.* Pitman Publishing, 1944.

Yenne, Bill. *The American Aircraft Factory in World War II.* Zenith Press, 2006.

I